My World
Your World

Time for School

by Ellen Lawrence

Ruby Tuesday Books

Published in 2015 by Ruby Tuesday Books Ltd.

Editor: Mark J. Sachner
Designer: Emma Randall
Production: John Lingham

Photo credits:
Alamy: Cover, 2, 5 (bottom left), 6–7, 9, 10 (center), 11 (bottom right), 14, 16, 20–21, 22; Corbis: 5 (top left), 10 (left), 22; FLPA: 8, 11 (left), 12–13, 17, 22; Getty Images: 15, 18–19, 22; Shutterstock: 4 (Pavel Svoboda), 10 (right), 11 (top right: arindambanerjee), 22, 23 (Pavel Svoboda); Superstock: 5 (right).

Library of Congress Control Number: 2014958141

ISBN 978-1-910549-04-9

Printed and published in the United States of America

For further information including rights and permissions requests, please contact our Customer Service Department at 877-337-8577.

The picture on the front cover of this book shows a classroom of children at school in China. Their school is in a village in the countryside. The school has just a small number of pupils.

Contents

Words shown in **bold** in the text are explained in the glossary.

All the places in this book are shown on the map on page 22.

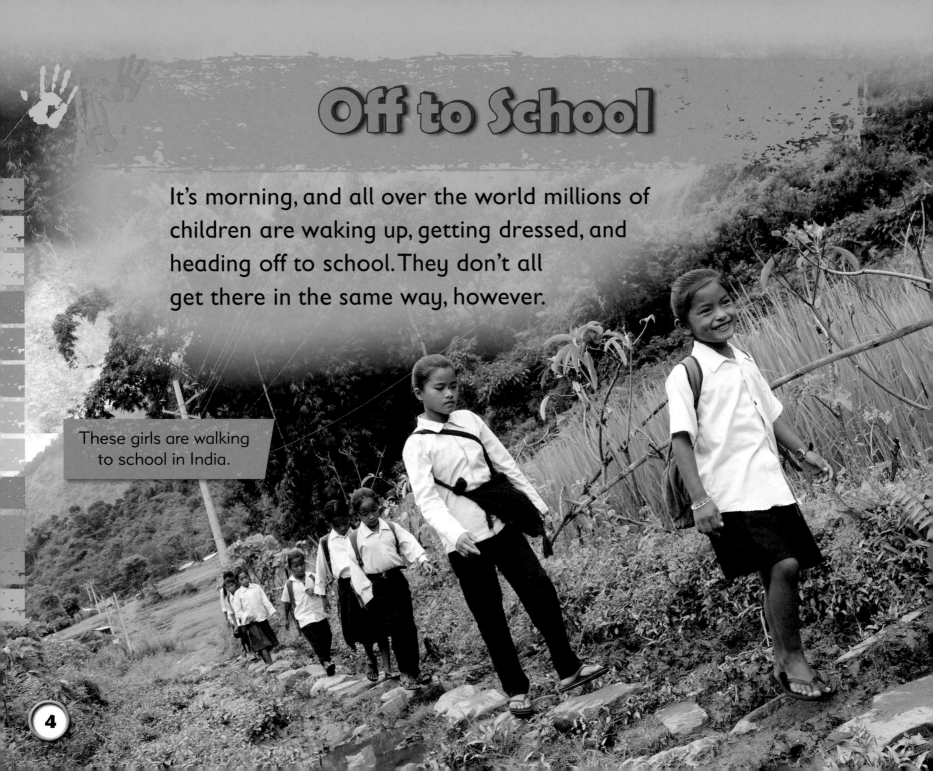

Off to School

It's morning, and all over the world millions of children are waking up, getting dressed, and heading off to school. They don't all get there in the same way, however.

These girls are walking to school in India.

A school bus in New York City

This small and overcrowded bus is carrying children to school in Indonesia.

On a school day in the United States and Canada, 30 million children ride to school on yellow buses.

These students in Myanmar travel to and from school by boat.

Our Classrooms

Once they get to school, kids settle down to work in their classrooms.

In Tanzania, these Maasai children study in a classroom that has a dirt floor and walls made out of branches.

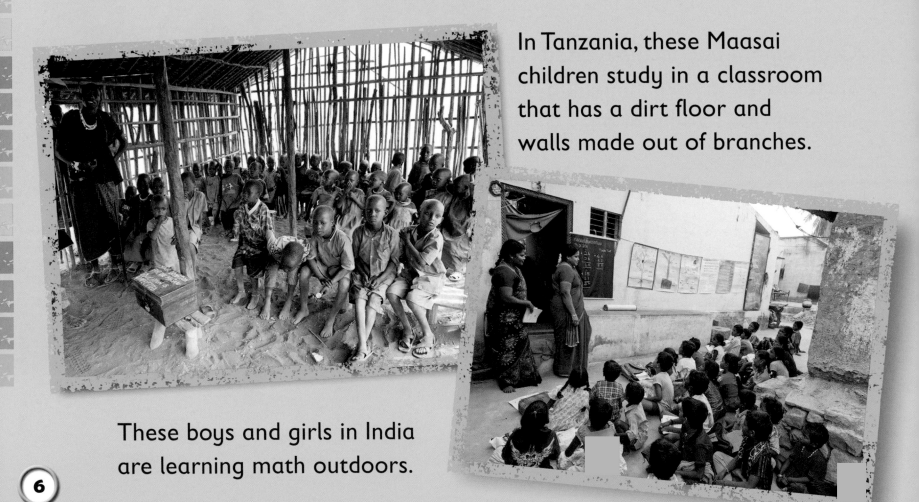

These boys and girls in India are learning math outdoors.

This classroom in Russia is decorated with balloons for the first day of the **term** in September. On this day, children bring flowers for their teachers. They also wear their best clothes, and girls wear large white bows in their hair.

A Very Tiny School

Off the coast of **mainland** Scotland is the tiny island of Canna. The island is home to one of the smallest elementary schools in the world.

Only a few families live on Canna.

So sometimes Canna School has just three or four pupils!

A farmhouse on Canna

Once children on Canna are 12 years old, they go to school on the mainland. The **ferry** journey can take nearly three hours. So children live at the school and only go home for the weekend every two weeks.

This photo shows four pupils and a teacher at Canna School in 2010.

The school building

What Do We Do at School?

We read and write and study math and science.

These Xingu (sheen-GOO) children in the Amazon rain forest are reading a book together.

Some children work on computers and tablets.

This girl in India does her schoolwork on a chalkboard.

We have fun making art.

These kids on the Falkland Islands have painted pictures of large seabirds called albatrosses. The birds come to the islands to lay eggs and raise their chicks.

We sing, make music, and dance.

We see our friends and favorite teachers.

The Camel Library

It's fun to go to the school library to choose a book. For some children who live in Kenya in Africa, the library has to come to them.

The camel library

Many people in Kenya are **nomads**.

They move from place to place with their animals.

Their small villages, or camps, are usually far from towns.

So a camel library visits the nomads' villages.

The camel library visits a school for nomad children.

A librarian, library assistants, and a camel herder travel with three camels. The animals carry about 200 books between them. The books are laid out on a mat on the ground so readers can make their choices.

13

Earthquake Drills

Japan is a country that has many **earthquakes**. During an earthquake, the ground shakes. This can cause terrible damage to buildings.

Japanese children hiding under desks

Most Japanese schools have an earthquake drill once a month.

This teaches children what to do in case of an earthquake.

To stay safe from falling walls or ceilings, children must hide under their desks.

They practice doing this during earthquake drills.

These kids are wearing padded fireproof hoods during an earthquake drill.

Buildings that are damaged by an earthquake may catch fire. So during an earthquake drill, children also prepare for fires breaking out. They practice taking different escape routes from their school.

Learning on Class Trips

Lots of learning goes on outside the classroom.

These children in England are on a class trip to a farm.

They are learning how sheep and cattle are raised for meat.

An elephant keeper

A two-month-old
elephant calf

In Africa,
thousands of adult
elephants are killed by
poachers each year. The
animals are killed for their
tusks. Elephants' tusks are made
of ivory, which is used to make
jewelry and ornaments. During
class trips to the center,
children learn about
protecting elephants.

These schoolchildren in Kenya are visiting a
center for baby elephants that have lost their mothers.

The mother elephants were killed by hunters called **poachers**.

The babies are raised by keepers at the center.

A School in a Tent

In 2011, a war began in Syria. Millions of Syrian people left their homes to escape from danger. These people became **refugees**.

Thousands of refugees found safety at the Al Zaatari refugee camp in Jordan.

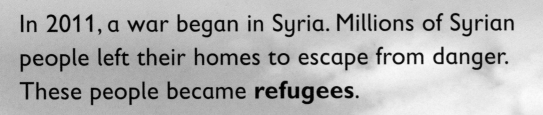

At the camp, some children get to go to school in tent classrooms.

A teacher at the camp rings the bell for school to start.

This tent classroom was set up by UNICEF, which is an organization that helps children.

On school days, children leave their tent homes. Then they walk through the large camp to their school. Girls have their lessons in the morning, and boys go to school in the afternoon.

No Time for School

Many children cannot go to school. This is because they have to go to work every day.

This girl in Peru earns money selling gum on the street.

Children work to earn money to help their families pay for food and medical care.

Thankfully, many people are trying to help working children.

One thing that can be changed is to make bosses pay adult workers higher wages.

If parents can earn more money, their children won't have to work.

In Cambodia, children work on garbage dumps. They collect plastic to sell to companies that recycle plastic. The garbage dumps are filthy, dangerous places, and they smell very bad. The children earn just a few cents for a whole day's work.

Where in the World?

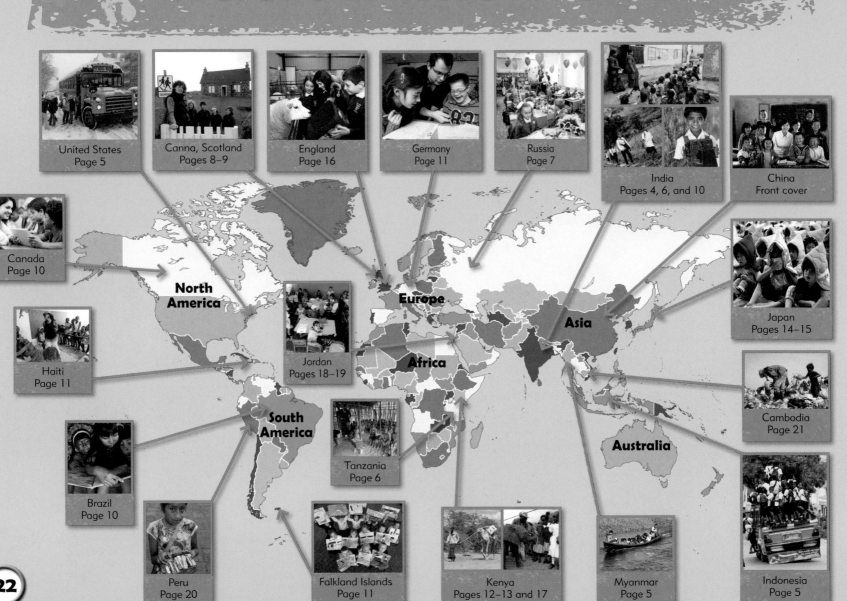

United States
Page 5

Canna, Scotland
Pages 8–9

England
Page 16

Germany
Page 11

Russia
Page 7

India
Pages 4, 6, and 10

China
Front cover

Canada
Page 10

North
America

Europe

Asia

Japan
Pages 14–15

Haiti
Page 11

Jordan
Pages 18–19

Africa

Cambodia
Page 21

Brazil
Page 10

South
America

Tanzania
Page 6

Australia

Peru
Page 20

Falkland Islands
Page 11

Kenya
Pages 12–13 and 17

Myanmar
Page 5

Indonesia
Page 5

22

Glossary

earthquake (URTH-kwake)
A sudden shaking caused by underground movements in Earth's outer layer, or crust.

ferry (FER-ee)
A boat that regularly carries people or vehicles from one place to another. A ferry is a little like a bus, except that it carries people over water instead of land.

mainland (MAYN-luhnd)
The largest and main part of a country. For example, Scotland is made up of a large mainland area and hundreds of small islands, including Canna. The islands are not joined to the mainland, but they are still part of Scotland.

nomad (NOH-mad)
A person who regularly moves from one area to another and does not live in one place all the time.

poacher (POH-chur)
A person who breaks the law by killing an animal or taking it from its natural habitat.

refugee (REF-yoo-jee)
A person who has been forced to leave his or her home to escape danger and needs to be protected.

term (TURM)
A period of time, which usually lasts for several weeks or months, during which children must go to school. Between each school term there are holiday and summer breaks.

Index

Read More

Chambers, Catherine. *School Days Around the World (DK Readers)*. New York: DK Publishing (2007).

Rice, Dona Herwick. *School Around the World (TIME for Kids)*. Huntington Beach, CA: Teacher Created Materials (2012).

Learn More Online

To learn more about schools around the world, go to
www.rubytuesdaybooks.com/school